The Abundant

...an enlightened ant colony pioneers a new
perspective on living

James Mackenzie Wright

Fisher King Publishing

For lovely Katy,
for bringing so many new layers of
abundance to my life.

Abundant : əˈbʌnd(ə)nt - adj.

Origin: a-bund-ant: First known usage – 150 million years ago

'A': determiner; indefinite article denoting one thing or group;

'Bund': noun; a tract of land or causeway often flanked by water;

'Ant': noun; a small insect living in a socially complex colony.

Meaning: bounteous, prolific, complete, and inexhaustible.

Contents

Part I

Tumultuous Times

Chapter 1 - Staying Alive

Simply staying alive was our primary instinct
in those early years. Without question, this was
a tumultuous time for our earliest ancestors, as
we made our logical but precarious evolution
from wasps. Thousands of disparate ant clans
were springing up all over the savannahs, each
competing for land and resources. Many of us
had started turning on each other, all angling for
superiority in our desperate quest for survival.
The resulting tensions threatened to wipe out huge
swathes of our emerging populations as ants from
all clans bickered and fought for security.

There was also the omnipresent threat of predation
from other animals and mammals - ('the gigantics'
as ants call them) - who were fast learning that a
large mouthful of us made a tasty meal, or who
were simply so indifferent to us that they thought
nothing of trampling on us and our nests if we
happened to be in their paths.

Several forward-thinking clans, believing that

safety in numbers would be advantageous, began merging to create the first known supercolony, which became known as the Coherant. Fortuitously, the Coherant founders had had the vision to secure an imposing position on an enormous, high rock outcrop which afforded valuable protection to all the inhabitants.

Despite this, inevitable difficulties presented themselves often. For every new migrant clan that found its own customs accepted by the supercolony, another encountered disapproval. The Coherant worked to soften the tensions and mediate the differences. The colony steadily grew and unified. Word spread quickly and thousands of ants and entire clans began to arrive asking for sanctuary.

Initially, the Coherant had attempted to welcome as many newcomers as possible. Over time though, their strong rope of compassion began to fray into fragile threads of misgiving. Nervous comparisons and judgments surfaced. Some migrants were adjudged to offer very little benefit to their host who had begun turning ants away at the frontiers, creating further tensions within the colony. However, given that it was, at that time, the only inclusive supercolony of its kind, the Coherant had become established as a safe, well-meaning, if mercurial refuge.

Chapter 2 - Anthea

Anthea was an inquisitive ant with a resolute belief in her own ability to make things happen. Arguably, this quality was predictable since her father and Queen both originated from the Endurant clan in the southern savannahs of Africa. One of the oldest and most distinguished clans then known to antkind, the Endurant were among the first to vote to inaugurate their entire clan into the Coherant supercolony.

Learned anthropologists had pinpointed areas in those same savannahs where they believed our original ancestors likely evolved. This information thrilled Anthea, because it provided her with an innate and enduring tie to all the earliest known clans and colonies that had evolved there.

At just three days old, a mere antling, Anthea was already recognised as a conspicuously bright scholar. Her instincts held an alarming precocity and she soon became a regular fixture at the debating chambers of the Antique - a contemplative society of elderly ants - who were at once intrigued (and later alarmed, as we shall see), at her incisive and outspoken points of view.

Our all-too-recent genesis had become a wondrous contemplation for her, and she was frequently to be found debating with the Antique on expansive issues; how, (and indeed why), ants had come into existence; how we might achieve a state of harmony alongside the gigantics; innovative survival philosophies we should be considering, and so on.

"We are still too small and exposed," she pronounced at one meeting. "All pioneer colonies will need to grow rapidly and find safer shelter in order to protect themselves and to self-sustain. Any nascent species must expect hardships and we ants are no different. In addition to predatory gigantics and inhospitable climatic and geographical conditions, we are warmongering and creating self-inflicted judgments too.

"All this jeopardises our chances of longevity,"

she noted. "The primary casualty will inevitably be our societal cohesion. If this falters, so too does our ability to present our front of impenetrability and we shall be less able to deter attack. If we, as Coherant, cannot assure safety through cohesion, what indeed is our colony purpose?"

The Antiques had to concede her point. Despite Anthea's comparative youth, the Antiques nominated her as their community strategist, since her ideas and arguments were far more structured - albeit more radical too - than any they had previously encountered. They believed themselves too old to create new, workable survival ideas, or to fight off invaders in the event of an attack. They had become resigned to a capricious undercurrent of fear which seemed to be growing in momentum throughout the colony, and fervently hoped she would be the ant who would somehow magick a utopian, peaceful society.

Anthea instinctively felt that societal cohesion and compassionate leadership would prove far more beneficial than military protection. She turned over her thoughts in her mind for days, knowing she must appear steadfast and prepared to defend her strategy under scrutiny from all directions.

She laid out her thoughts to the Antiques in her customary no-nonsense manner: "Building an inclusive social mindset will become our best asset. I propose we should quickly attract even more ants from hundreds, thousands maybe, of like-minded clans whose appetite for communal survival is as raw and insatiable as our own."

"We accept your suggestion for safety in numbers," said one Antique, "but you are asking us to unite many more clans who already live by their own customs. What of them? How can we expect them to accept leadership from us, who to them are relative strangers?"

"First and foremost, we are all ants. Brethren and sistren. Family," replied Anthea firmly. "Word will spread that we have created a secure and organised colony at a time when almost none exist," she continued. "Not only that, but that we Coherant are thriving and looking to extend our influence to the advantage of all antkind. We shall blend the most beneficial customs from all the arriving immigrants into one distinct and peaceable philosophy. And then scale up to create a second supercolony, a third, and many, many more in the same design."

The Antiques shifted uneasily from foot to foot. "Is this though, just idle reverie, Anthea?" they asked. "Whilst we commend your optimism, we are concerned that this colony (or any of our future colonies) could easily be over-run by ants purely looking for a safe haven, with little interest in contributing positively for our collective good."

"How does it serve us," another asked, "to simply give shelter and food to those who might give nothing back?"

Their concerns amplified. "Are we, indeed, strong enough to face all the difficulties of growing and protecting a rapidly growing new supercolony?"

"And where would we find the knowledge to do this?"

"And how will we be able to communicate such a vision to these immigrants?"

"How would we, an ageing population, defend ourselves, if some aggressive factions joined our colony, with the aim of attacking us from within?"

"Who will lead this initiative? And how? How can we convince so many diverse cultures to accept one path?"

The questions continued.

Anthea understood that their disquiet was genuine and valid. "I note your anxieties around the consequences of opening up our colonies to unknowns," she admitted. "It is natural to have misgivings about things we have not yet experienced. Truthfully, I cannot yet answer all your questions myself yet, but this I know: we are living with a siege mentality. Our mindset is geared only to survival. My proposal is that we work to grow past this current mindset and construct a new one that provides opportunity, contentment and confidence rather than judgement, anxiety and blame. I sense our thinking will advance organically if we are open to it."

She paused to reflect before continuing firmly. "I sense that this does not have to become the 'idle reverie' of which you speak. I sense too that the essence of being an ant lives within our resourcefulness. I have a profound and unshakeable trust that we shall find ants who know these things. Then we shall invite them to talk with us."

The Antiques looked to each other. "We appreciate your candour," one noted. "So, perhaps you could now spell out exactly what you propose for our continued security and well-being. And more pertinently, how precisely we should achieve it?"

Chapter 3 - Anthea's vision

Anthea recognised that this was a defining moment. She had harboured these thoughts for so long inside her mind that it seemed impossible that they could be received badly. Here was her chance. She breathed deeply several times, looked directly at the assembled Antiques, and began.

"Esteemed colleagues. We are Coherant. We purport to value togetherness. In togetherness lies strength. Until now we have been selective in our invitations. Here is our opportunity - our biggest yet - to open our minds and our arms and fully embrace all antkind. Every ant, every clan, every culture will be welcomed at our frontiers.

"Long ago, our Coherant ancestors understood they should define a common identity for the colony," she reminded them. "Their reasoning remained as acute today as it did then; when we know what we stand for, we can better understand our ambition and purpose, and work towards it. And so, they creatcd our Charter based on safety in numbers and strength in togetherness. The idea of the supercolony was…"

"Anthea," interrupted an Antique, gently, "we are all aware of our Charter, as you well know. Togetherness, connection and collaboration has always been our truth, and this has been tested countless times over countless generations. We are all in agreement that we must remain clear on our identity, our ambition and our purpose going forward. We have welcomed innumerable migrants, over many generations. We have pioneered and shaped this supercolony as our ideal.

"Our ancestors probably didn't envisage how large we might eventually become. Well, this is the challenge we now face - how much bigger can we become before cracks appear? And then how long before those cracks widen and become serious rifts? And you are asking that we welcome… every ant that shows up at our frontier?! We are already the most diverse colony we know of.

"So, our questions to you remain unanswered: what

do you propose we actually do to move forward? And how?"

Anthea took more deep breaths. Her proposal was risky, untested and purely intuitive.

"I am voting in favour of a peaceable policy. My vision appears (to me at least) to be simple," she told the Antiques. "I recommend that we forego our traditional stance of aggressive deterrence. We already have a sizeable number of militants we can call on within the colony, if we need them. But in spite of these, if we are ever attacked, we would be hard pushed to provide a guarantee of safety to our inhabitants. We just don't know what others' capabilities might be.

"Next, as I stated before, I recommend that we renounce our siege mindset. It is holding us back. We need to find a more forward-looking, expansive mindset to live up to. We certainly need to understand the nature of our current mindset, and how productive or otherwise it might actually be.

"So how might we do this? My initial proposal is

that we can first audit all our Coherant inhabitants to find out more about their own approaches to survival, but also what more, if anything, they might be wishing to replace it with. Then we can travel out to the savannahs to understand how other clans and colonies are living and where their own ambitions and talents lie. There will doubtless be huge fields of new and exciting information we can observe and study. From this, we can design new, bespoke lifestyle strategies, just how we want them.

"To achieve this, we will also need to create an even wider sense of inclusion. We need to embed a perception of contentment and prosperity at levels so high as to eclipse any craving for conflict. We want to encourage would-be allies and enemies alike to find their own elevation and spread the word to others. They can do this by joining us rather than fighting us. When our colony has become safe, strong and self-sufficient, we can begin to scale up and build new ones in the same blueprint." She paused.

"Anthea, as you know, we have many disparate

clans living amongst us within this very Coherant supercolony," one Antique stated, solemnly.

"Many of them are likely retaining aspects of their previous customs and disciplines, despite living as Coherant. These are mostly known to us, even if we don't share them. But outside our boundaries - are you aware of the dangers and chaos that exists out there on the savannahs? These are unknowns. There is no precedent for achieving a plan like this. How would we even start?"

"Precedents are a luxury to be earned over time," replied Anthea evenly. We ants are a new species - we have not yet had time to achieve anything of note. In time, I wish for us a mindset that doesn't contain a need for survival. But currently our siege instinct is as intense as it is resourceful. I concede that can also be seen as a strength. However, you talk of danger. That is possible. You mention chaos. That is probable. But in chaos lives hope. In hope lives resolve. In resolve lives action. And in our actions, I am persuaded, we shall find the guidance we need."

The Antiques looked to one another. Anthea continued quickly, before they had a chance to counter her arguments.

"I repeat, once we, the Coherant have redefined our mindset to represent all that is optimal and aspirational, we can scale up and bring unity and cohesion colony by colony to all antkind. My guess, like yours, I imagine, is that it will not be an easy transition to achieve and that many struggles lie ahead of us. However, something so magnificent and enduring is most definitely worth the crusade."

Such was her conviction and boldness. Disarming and forthright as ever. Anthea looked around her. The Antiques were visibly anxious and unsettled. Their mood was pensive.

Anthea was in no mood to be deterred. "If you would like some fresh thinking, let me suggest we call for the Consultant to shine some light on the matter."

The Antiques appeared relieved to have the opportunity to hear a new voice and several ants from the Consultant were duly summoned.

Chapter 4 - The Consultant

Methodical and assured as usual, the Consultant laid out their thoughts.

"To accomplish Anthea's vision, you would need to create a vast, all-inclusive population of peaceful, motivated and productive ants, large enough to deter any would-be attackers while simultaneously building robust societal structures," they proclaimed.

"Word will soon get out that you are building a safe and prosperous community. We propose a three-step approach. The first step is to hold interviews with every single Coherant in the colony. Depending on the outcome of that canvass, you can decide whether to take a second step: to build a more expansive outreach programme and canvass a much wider population out there on the savannahs. As your third step, you might then choose to issue open invitations to any migrants that wish to inaugurate."

The Antiques were aghast. "Interviews with every Coherant? And then with every new itinerant, migrant or vagrant that shows up seeking refuge? Every single one? We would be overwhelmed! And over-run! Building an inclusive Coherant lifestyle has always been our priority, but with those potential numbers arriving at our frontiers … why, they might be totally out of step with our ways of thinking. How would we possibly manage a process like that?"

"Every single one," affirmed the Consultant. "Be resolute, esteemed Friends. Be bold. And let's be cautious against making shallow assumptions about others' suitability, or their intentions or motives, for joining you. Open minds open doors. Behind those doors may lie a magic we might otherwise be denied."

Anthea was smiling. "This is precisely what I envision," she said. "We only have to look around us at the wonderful, emotionally articulate souls we have attracted already. So many of our own immediate ancestors arrived as immigrants.

Including my own. We have learned that wisdom and genius manifests from unexpected sources, often from where one assumes there may be none. Others' diversities, life skills and experiences will serve to define and enhance all of us."

"We concur," nodded the Consultant. "Let your Coherant colony become a pilgrimage for all ants from far and wide seeking safety and a place to thrive."

"Yes, Friends. Soon, Coherant colonies can spring up everywhere," insisted Anthea. "I believe that the vast majority of migrants and their clans will want to integrate seamlessly and gratefully with us. Inevitably a number of them may need to be given suggestions as to how they might make small concessions to their behaviours and lifestyles. And some - (very few I hope) - may possibly need to be given encouragement to fully rethink their outlook on inclusive social living and reapply later. That said, I propose we let it be known that admittance to Coherant colonies will never be permanently refused to any ant."

"A wise and considered course of action,"
agreed the Consultant. They and Anthea looked
expectantly towards the Antiques.

The Antiques, however, were less enthusiastic.
"These are not lightweight matters, Anthea, and we
must discuss the consequences at length. We will
need time to confer - please be patient with us and
we will give you our answer this evening."

Anthea paced through the chambers. Her heart told
her that her proposal was the right one, though she
understood the risks to the colony. The Antiques
returned more quickly than expected. A bad sign?
A good sign? Anthea forced herself to remain
optimistic.

"Anthea, we applaud your vision and energies,
and we share your pragmatic outlook," said the
Antiques. "But we repeat - neither you nor the
Consultant have yet demonstrated how it can be
supported and sustained in the longer term. And
crucially, you have yet to propose who would know
how to execute such a complex project.

"For our part, we have talked with our militants, and they are adamant that the savannahs are too dangerous, currently, for us to be able to live safely with anything less than an imposing and conspicuous military presence. Even that may not be sufficient if we were attacked from all sides at once.

"You provide no demographics, no strategy, no guarantee of any kind," they continued. "If we were to accept your proposal, we would need, at the very least, a profile of the migrants we might expect to arrive. Even then, we may have to reject your vision. Be aware there are several reluctants among us - these are our lives and our livelihoods we are considering here."

As Anthea considered her next thought, the Consultant intervened, pragmatically.

"Esteemed Antiques, these are difficult decisions to make. However, to do nothing at all could result in the disintegration of everything you have worked for. It could put all your lives in far more acute danger than we experience now. We know just the clan to help you design and implement such a momentous social framework, and to bring all the pieces together," they said, with their hallmark conviction. "We recommend the ever-reliable Providant."

Chapter 5 - The Providant

A deputation of Providant arrived the following day. They were excited. After their briefing by Anthea and the Consultant, they immediately saw the benefits not solely of creating, but also of belonging to such a hybrid colony. They had proved themselves to be a studious, courageous, and dependable clan, with a devotion to building sustainable communities.

They were acutely aware that Anthea's proposition heralded a crucial juncture in the inception of antkind. Nothing of this sort or scale had ever been attempted before.

Naturally, they accepted the challenge. They spoke to the assembled ants.

"Fellow ants, at the conclusion of this task, you envisage building numerous Coherant supercolonies, wherein all inhabitants can exist in peace, contentment, and prosperity. You want to banish the turmoil and uncertainties that imperil your daily lives. As you are aware, the realisation of this task could become an historic moment for ants. Achieving it creates both disquiet and exhilaration in equal measure for us Providant.

"Disquiet, because we are well aware of the tempestuous and warlike origins of some clans who might seek to inaugurate as Coherant. Conversely… enormous exhilaration too. What a distinct privilege to be chosen to explore the social workings of a supercolony. What a monumental legacy to antkind! This is a complex undertaking of colossal proportions, and we commit to leave no stones unturned in our quest to complete it. We are humbled by the honour accorded to us and we relish and respect the opportunity. In addition, you may be sure we shall pledge ourselves and every ant from our own clan, without hesitation, as inaugurants to the new-look supercolony when it is finalised.

"We are mindful too, of the Antiques' reservations about sustainability and support. We are convinced that we must all fully understand the components of true community thinking, both within the Coherant boundaries and beyond. To accomplish this, we will first need to be aware of the behaviours and leadership strategies that the wider community of Coherant are adopting.

"Only then can we decide on whether we may need to research what is happening elsewhere. With all this knowledge we can build the frameworks we need to bond our progressive supercolony once and for all time. But without it, longer-term survival seems terribly uncertain."

The Providant bowed and stepped back.

The Consultant looked to each other and to Anthea for a few moments, nodding sagely. "What the Providant are suggesting requires the creation of a radical, robust and rigorous social framework to support Anthea's vision," they said. "Its purpose would be to protect and sustain all Coherant colonies as they proliferate across the savannahs and beyond. We believe this is the right course of action. It will likely require an intricate, risky, and lengthy intervention, involving thousands of volunteers. All that said, we feel that by not acting decisively, your eventual risk will be higher."

The Antiques looked to one another nervously. They conferred hastily, and one stepped forward to deliver their verdict.

"Very well. We shall agree, with conditions, to the domestic interviews and… yes, to the external outreach initiative too, if it should be deemed absolutely necessary. We insist on your guarantee that you can fully resource this venture without leaving the colony depleted, exposed, or otherwise at undue risk. On this condition we are adamant. If you convince us that these requirements can be satisfied, then we acquiesce, cautiously, to your proposition. Then we can see how we may proceed from there."

Anthea was overjoyed. She looked first to the Providant, then to the Consultant. She found no words in that moment, so, keeping (as best she could) a solemn expression on her face, she simply bowed to the Antiques, turned on her heels and left the chamber.

Chapter 6 - Planning

Later that evening, Anthea and the Providant set up their planning hub deep under the roots of a baobab, where they and their teams remained for several days and nights. There they designed the outreach itinerary that would eventually allow them to meet and learn from millions of other ants.

They immediately agreed to recruit a nomadic clan, the Antenna, whose geographical knowledge was widely respected. They tasked them first to create an accurate map of the Coherant colony boundaries, which was no small feat in itself, so widely had the colony grown across the rock outcrop. No one knew exactly how many Coherants existed, nor exactly how or with whom they might be living, since new migrants arrived weekly seeking refuge.

The Antenna's second task was to scout and provide accessible routes into and across the savannahs, in the event the Providant decided that more comprehensive analysis was necessary. Familiarity with the terrain would be essential;

anything less would be dangerous.

Next, they enlisted hundreds of volunteers and assistants, whose role would be to travel across the Coherant outcrop, and later, across the savannahs, meeting and talking with as many Coherants, new clans and colonies as they could find. Their mission: to attempt to understand and classify an enormous cross-section of antkind; their social structures, outlooks, their interactions, abilities and lifestyles.

The domestic audit took many weeks to complete, and the results were interesting but inconclusive. The Providant discovered a few significant differences, but by and large, an unexpectedly high number of Coherant revealed broadly similar mindsets, despite the diverse influx of migrants they represented. It was pleasing to note that the CoherAnt values and principles were being largely respected.

It wasn't long before Anthea and the Providant realised they would have to widen the outreach to the savannahs after all, to find more diversity of thought and a less homogenous outlook.

Wherever possible, the Providant's plan was to send volunteers outside the known safety areas and colonies to see where similarities and differences in survival behaviours might appear. They knew that these observations would likely be fraught with danger. Understandably, many of these external clans and colonies were barely functional given the unstable and tempestuous lifestyles they were obliged to lead.

"It will likely now become a lengthy and painstaking strategy," the Providant concluded. "We know full well that to closely observe the lifestyles and survival interactions of millions of unknown ants will be an ambitious undertaking. We will begin further recruitment and training for our huge band of volunteers without delay."

The role of the Antenna would become increasingly vital in helping locate the most populous colonies in regions right across the southern tip of Africa and gauging their approximate sizes. Volunteers would visit the closest and largest of these first to compile the most data most quickly. Following this, they would pause briefly to refine their interview techniques and then visit the smaller and more distant colonies to get the fullest perspectives possible.

It was agreed that a small cohort of volunteers would approach each clan and colony boundary, so as not to present a perceived threat to the inhabitants. Even this strategy was highly precarious. The volunteers would be trained to reveal just enough of Anthea's vision to gauge a useable reaction. Revealing too much might compromise the lightly protected Coherant, leaving them open to attack. Revealing too little might create suspicion or refusal of admittance.

Once the trust of the elders had been gained, the volunteers would ask to stay several days within each colony to talk with the inhabitants. They would ask them to reveal the survival tactics they considered important. They would be trained to look for successful colony-building innovations as well as for insights into the probable causes of communication breakdowns. They would chronicle every response and emotion closely.

The Providant foresaw that the travelling cohorts would need to renew and sustain strong, motivated teams of volunteers during the outreach mission, since it was inevitable that it could cover numerous ant generations. A normal lifespan for an ant can be months and years, although for the majority of worker ants, it can often be measured in just days and weeks. Hundreds of Queen ants were therefore recruited into the cohorts to replenish and maintain the volunteer numbers. As soon as new ants were born, they too would be trained and deployed during the mission.

All volunteers fully understood the importance and also the dangers of such an undertaking. They understood too, that for many of them it might well be the last time they would see the inside of a friendly colony. All possible risks of their endeavour; violence, assault, even death had to be anticipated. And yet the pull of being part of such a momentous chapter in the early history of antkind was so compelling that they readily accepted the risks and hardship.

Several days later, under the reassuring glow of the African dawn, a vast cohort of volunteers left the confines of the Coherant colony, excited to be changing the future of antkind forever.

Chapter 7 - A Meeting of Minds

Weeks passed, and then months. Steadily, meticulously, the volunteers chronicled the daily social interactions of millions of ants in their colonies and clans. The intelligence was continuously relayed back to Anthea and the Providant. At last, Anthea signalled that they had enough information and sent word via teams of itinerants that all volunteers were to return and report. It took several days for all the outreach volunteers to return from the savannahs. They were greeted excitedly by their hosts and then allowed time to rest.

The Providant command team convened a debate to be attended by the entire Coherant supercolony. Anthea opened the meeting.

"Esteemed Antiques, Coherant and fellow visionaries," she began. "It has been a long time since last we all were together and we recognise the sense of unease you have endured during this absence. You have waited patiently to hear how all our lives might be irrevocably changed.

"It is true we had anticipated that our volunteers would have to endure a wide range of physical dangers inherent in this volatile social landscape. They had prepared themselves to be compassionate out there, and to make sense of the complex mental processes and interactions between all the ants they would likely meet. They also have encountered situations they had never expected nor planned for, and sadly, many of our volunteers gave their lives for the information we are about to present to you. To use this information wisely is to honour their sacrifice.

"What they discovered, out there across the savannahs and here within our own boundaries, were interesting fragmentations amongst our antkin.

"From the interviews and observations they have carried out amongst countless clans and colonies, they noted eight distinct behavioural patterns. I shall now ask the Providant to present these in more detail. From our initial analysis we are confident we will be able to use and adapt these behaviours in various ways for our own community benefit, while continuing to welcome as many ants as want to join our number.

"Once the Providant have finished their presentation we invite all of you to move to discussion and debate to enhance our understanding and acceptance of the vision we intend to create for ourselves. We hope that this experience will encourage you all to share our belief that we can indeed adapt and use this information to build and grow."

A young Providant stepped forward. She waited for the assembled ants to settle.

"Esteemed friends. Anthea's prologue is as exciting as it is accurate," she began. Our first objective was, as you know, to better understand the Coherant mindset as it appears today. Our second was to see how you compare with the wider population outside your boundaries. And thirdly, once this information is established, we intend to make recommendations as to how best to take the colony forward in the safest and most productive way.

"It will come as no surprise to you all that our conclusion on the Coherant mindset is that it - as Anthea has hinted - is indeed currently rooted in siege mode. However, probably thanks to your heritage, encompassing many generations as an inclusive supercolony, your collective outlook is more expansive, forward-looking and optimistic than the vast majority of colonies we encountered.

"Your current desire to create robust community structures and leadership frameworks immediately sets you apart from the rest. It was already an exciting privilege to be able to tour within your own colony boundaries and to meet so many of you. Despite many of you having originated from other clans, bringing many diverse ideas and cultures with you, it is gratifying to see how you have all embraced a unified Coherant outlook.

"We are pleased that you have been able to make and find the lives you are searching for, here, within the Coherant supercolony. Having seen so many diverse and extreme approaches to survival outside your boundaries, it is doubly impressive to note the contributions you all make to provide healthy and productive lives for each other.

"On our second phase, as we travelled across the enormous savannahs, we observed that the huge majority of ants we encountered were typically inclined towards the baser and more desperate siege behaviours that we shall share with you shortly.

"That said, all of us here, ourselves included of course, will likely recognise ourselves in one or perhaps more of these eight siege behaviours. No doubt these are innate mechanisms of ensuring safety and we should certainly accept them readily, and work with them creatively.

"We encountered numerous clans outside the Coherant boundaries in the wild savannahs. Regardless of their lifestyles, they, like us, are all doing their level best just to survive and to provide for their own colonies in these turbulent times. There is not an ant among us who does not identify with this situation.

"We concede that there currently exist a number of, shall we say, raw behaviours - what you may perceive as potentially unhelpful or destructive aspects of some of these behaviours and attitudes - but please try to look past them for now. We ask you not to judge, since these are doubtless fuelled by the fear and uncertainty that exists out there.

"There is much we can learn from these behaviours. We find them to be elaborate yet basic. They are instinctual yet considered. We appreciate that they do not, as yet, represent the polished community leadership framework that we are all searching for. But that too, will come. We are certain that with patience and kindness they can be modified and harmonised into durable and acceptable social structures that we can all live by.

"Excuse me, but why do you feel the need for all

this long-winded justification?" interrupted an ant from the crowd.

"That's a good point," called another. Up to now you are not exactly 'selling' us these potential immigrants in a very positive light."

"Permit me then to move to my presentation and I hope you may find answers to your questions," replied the Providant, evenly. "We have given titles to each siege behaviour and a summary of their qualities to make them easier for you to identify with."

Chapter 8 - Survival Behaviour

"So, as Anthea has mentioned," the Providant continued, "from our observations and interviews it seems that ants with similar behaviours and perspectives towards survival have begun to band together in order to give themselves more security and deepen their own convictions.

"In all cases, these behaviours derive from a very basic need to survive. We have talked with these ants, lived amongst them, and we know that deep down they are seeking the same lives as we are; safe, productive and carefree.

"We have identified four different perspectives within the siege conditions experienced by the ants. Some ants felt **exposed** and vulnerable; some were attempting to take **control** of their lives and those of others; some were committed to **growth** and building a better situation; the others were **accepting** of whatever life brought to them.

"Within those four siege perspectives we found

dozens of coping tactics and behaviours that the ants had learned or nurtured, just to survive each day's uncertainties. These mostly fell into eight distinct groups of survival behaviours:

"There are the **Truants** and **Dissonants**, (who held the *exposed* perspective),

The **Dominants** and **Savants** (who sought to *control* whatever they could),

Then the **Exuberants** and **Brilliants** (who decided that *growth* was their best survival offering),

And lastly the **Servants** and **Vibrants** (who were calmly *accepting* of the way things were).

"Let me outline the characteristics of each in some more detail, and you can take a view on how they might benefit our colony, were they to join us."

***

The Vibrants

"First, the **Vibrants**, whom we found typifying the

Accepting perspective. Their attitude to survival actually seemed to be extremely principled and virtuous. They displayed a remarkable lack of concern about any personal dangers they might face. They conveyed a belief that the inherent goodness and wisdom of all ants will triumph over any adversity when the conditions become right.

"They seemed to model flexibility, calm, cheerfulness, levity and a laudable serenity which was as effortlessly kind as it was gracious. They exuded an empowering empathic detachment. There was never a hint of judgment or blame in their language, and they confronted others' dilemmas, challenges, successes and achievements uniformly with imperturbability, assurance and worldliness.

"They spoke succinctly and listened keenly - their ability to detach from the dramas and dilemmas is obviously intentional, coming as it does from a deep belief in the ability of others to find their own solutions to life. Their style was to question rather than offer advice. They appeared to exhibit a boundless sense of belief and trust in others, encouraging the infinite potential of all those around them to show itself and take root in action…"

"Excuse me for interrupting," called an ant from the middle of the chamber. "Although this sounds a commendable way to live one's life, is it actually very… productive? I for one wouldn't mind inviting ants like these into our colony, but as workers, they don't seem very… dynamic."

"You make a fair point," responded the Providant. "This question-mark about their suitability for hard, physical work has been noted. I should add, however, that we detected very little animosity towards the Vibrants from other ants. Any criticism there may have been, seemed to originate from them being perceived as overly spiritual and perhaps a little distant."

"These points aside, however, the Vibrants collectively presented themselves as holistic, wise, calm, compassionate, mature, alert, trusting, warm and likeable ants to have around."

"They certainly seem like decent ants to live alongside. They'd get my vote," called out a voice from the crowd.

"Thank you," smiled the Providant. "Let me continue with a summary of all the groups, and we can discuss whatever we need to at the end."

The Servants

"We named the next group the **Servants**, also in the **Accepting** category. They were studiously supportive and unselfish. They manifested this by inviting self-awareness and self-discovery in those around them, rather than by providing hasty solutions or being 'the reason' for others' successes.

"It's evident they were naturally very perceptive and successful when it came to siege tactics. Consistency and even-handedness were key characteristics we observed in Servants and they had developed a mindset of service to others. They were attentive and considerate and had developed a very natural, relational approach by mirroring others' words and energies back to them - a generous and effective way of bestowing insights and understanding. Their maturity seemed to be born of a deep knowledge and acceptance of self, without feeling the need to over-empathise as a means of creating trust and rapport.

"We occasionally noticed their commendable patience becoming fazed by the irrational behaviour of others, and we observed an occasional inclination to be judgmental, which, to their credit, they worked hard to suppress. However, their powerful instinct for self-examination recreates a mature, supportive perspective and they are very forgiving of themselves and others. It is obvious they have worked hard on themselves to be able to interact at this level of acceptance of the world around them.

"On the down-side, we noted some ants having difficulty relating to this and as a consequence, the Servants occasionally found themselves shunned and misunderstood by those who were intimidated by their aura of exemplariness. Broadly speaking, they appeared to be fair-minded, self-confident, reliable, cultured, impartial, unselfish, reflective and sincere."

"So far so good," shouted a voice from the crowd.

"Yes, but can they actually do anything? Like, proper, hard work for us?" retorted another.

"You don't need to continue with the rest - let's just invite these two groups in now, and close our boundaries for a while!" called out a third.

The Providant smiled. "We'd be happy to explore that possibility in due course, for sure. We would like to give you a much wider flavour of all the various survival behaviours beforehand though," she said patiently. "May we ask that you hear the full presentation before discussions begin? There are six more to introduce to you. Shall I continue?"

The Providant took a moment to observe the expectant faces of the ants in front of her and then calmly resumed.

The Brilliants

"The next group I'd like to introduce you to are the the **Brilliants**. They definitely hold the **Growth** perspective. Their survival attitude was more altruistic and outward looking, and they seemed to be constantly searching for new ways to ease and enhance the conditions in which we all live.

"The Brilliants seemed to be the most pragmatic of all the groups, and particularly so in crisis situations. They assumed credibility as leaders by demonstrating their wide breadth of creativity and initiative. Their approach to survival was simple: by viewing their surroundings as a blank canvas, upon which to innovate their ingenious ideas, they made themselves relevant, appreciated and therefore, they hoped, indispensable.

"They most definitely preferred talking to listening, however, and appeared generally forthright, blunt and unafraid to make mistakes (which, from their rather self-important viewpoint, they inevitably saw as necessary stepping stones in any creative process). Their minds worked with an awesome agility and speed, which meant they could rarely listen to the end of others' sentences before concluding it in their own way, or relating it to their own experiences.

"We perceived that they weren't interrupting to be rude, but more to be expansive and exploratory. Either way, we heard accusations from other ants of their egotism, impatience and arrogance. In the same vein, their energies, passions, versatility and ingenuity were so compelling, that others often found them exhausting and over-confident.

"All that said, we found the Brilliants to be alluring, bold, optimistic, persistent, inventive, daring, resourceful, engaging, feisty and very, very bright."

"Well, they sound interesting too - we could certainly use some sharp brains like that," called out an ant from the crowd.

"They actually sound draining to me," said another. "Just the opposite of those first two. I don't know if I could handle having ants with all that energy around me all the time!"

"It's true they sometimes over-rely on their charisma," agreed the young Providant. "And here's another stimulating group with the Growth perspective we have named the Exuberants - see what you think of them."

The Exuberants

"We found **Exuberants** were fun to have around since they held that everything is not as bad as it appears and that there is humour and levity just about everywhere. Like the Brilliants they held a **Growth** outlook, with an emphasis less on innovation and more on raising morale. And unlike the Brilliants, the Exuberants were very good at listening, patiently waiting for the full extent of others' views to become apparent, (although with a tendency to find a mischievous angle to alter the perspective from time to time).

"They fell easily into self-deprecation and didn't mind looking foolish if it was pleasing to their audience. They were caring and supportive and instinctively knew when to put on a serious face, although behind that mask they were likely weighing up what they could be saying to lighten a situation.

"They believe that facts and logic are, shall we say, arbitrary concepts and shouldn't necessarily be allowed to dampen or stifle a fun story. It was not uncommon that they voiced their thoughts before fully distilling what might have been a more appropriate or socially correct response. For that reason other ants tended to find them a little disrespectful, superficial or trivial, causing issues of distrust.

"Typically, they were indecisive and preferred to sit on the fence in debates, constantly wary of the reactions of their audience. They showed no desire to promote themselves as an authority on any serious issue, and, faced with dissent, they'd recoil into jokiness and levity so as not to be taken over-seriously.

"We found them to be charming, spontaneous, motivational, uplifting, quirky, roguish, tantalising, zany but also slightly superficial and tricky on occasion."

"Yes, yes, but are you sure we need that level of frivolity?" called out an elderly Coherant, impatiently. "This is a time for re-thinking our whole way of life. It is not a time for jokery."

"I'm not sure I completely agree with you, Colleague, though I respect your concern," countered the Providant. "Our contention is that we too are likely to find our own behaviours reflected in any one of these siege approaches, including this one. Many ants are creating an unmistakeable survival presence for themselves by being jokey, shallow or eccentric it's true, although we also recognised their intention as being more motivational and uplifting. We enjoyed their company, all things considered. Who among us perhaps recognises traits like these in ourselves, or among our friends?"

The elderly Coherant remained silent, and the assembled ants murmured to each other. "You may have a point," called out one. "Let's hear about the rest then."

The Savants

"Another group of clans had found one another through a far more intellectual approach. We named them the **Savants** and they were quick to share their outlook on survival, from a more **Controlling** perspective. "We make life work for us by knowing more than anyone else," they told us. "Ants respect knowledge, and if we show ourselves to be more knowledgeable than others, we become essential - they will need to keep us around."

"For Savants, like the Exuberants, dialogue also genuinely meant listening to others' points of view. This again, appeared to be a positive step, although the Savants became 'preachy' quite often and would steer others' points of view towards their own decorous rules and lofty social protocols.

"Generally, Savants were articulate and capable and

held an educated view about most topics. If they had no previous opinions on a topic they instantly put their mind to it and created one, believing that a healthy mind is an agile mind. They were very decisive, and confidently believed they occupied the moral and cultural 'high ground'.

"Once in their flow, they came across as expert, cultured, intellectual, engaging, credible, cautious and hard-working, but, it must be said, also as fussy, high-brow, stubborn, self-righteous and judgmental."

"Well, education is one thing, and a superiority complex is another. I'm not sure I would put up with those sorts of behaviours for very long," called out an ant from the audience.

"I agree, these Savants are starting to sound a bit full of their own importance," said another, "I'm not sure they would be a welcome addition to any colony."

"Educated or not, self-important or not, let me ask for your patience, Colleagues," soothed the

Providant. "The Savants are indeed a complex group, with many intriguing traits. In their own way they are Controllers as we mentioned. We observed them being straightforward, amicable and articulate on one hand, although touchy and pompous on another. And much more besides, certainly. But remember, let's look around us, (and within ourselves too, perhaps?) In which of these behavioural groups might each one of us really find ourselves too, deep down? Which of these behaviours might we most naturally adopt when a dangerous moment arrives?"

The young Providant paused to allow her questions to fully sink in. She was expecting more resistance, but the assembled Coherant appeared to be mulling over this academic standpoint.

"There are still three behaviours left to highlight," she continued carefully. "There is much to learn from all this diversity, and many insights we believe we can use to shape our new colonies. Please allow me to give you the fullest picture of all approaches before we debate our future actions.

May I continue?"

The Coherants looked to one another and nodded.

The Dominants

"Our next group's siege tactics were, on the face of it… a little more concerning. We have named them the **Dominants**…"

There was a collective, puzzled gasp from the audience.

The Providant took a breath and continued. "I earlier flagged up that some characteristics and antalities may appear less palatable than others. As I present these last three groups to you, I can understand how they may well seem edgier and less obviously productive to you than the previous…"

"Edgier? Less productive?" interrupted an Antique. "I was waiting for you to get to this group. 'Dominants'? You're going to ask us to accept aggression and strong-arm tactics now, aren't you? And there are still two more groups to come after this, the… well, what are you calling them again?"

"Well, the groups after this one we have named the Dissonants and Truants, and I will come to them shortly," replied the Providant, trying not to show the nervousness she was suddenly feeling.

"Right. Dissonants and Truants. So we have to welcome them too, do we? They already sound surplus to requirements to me. I'm not convinced we need to invite any more low-performing groups of ants. Do any of them actually do any work? At a pinch we might be able to accommodate some of the ants you have highlighted already, although even that could be a stretch. Some might potentially contribute some positive nuance to our colony but I think I've heard enough. Who's with me?"

Many ants nodded their agreement.

But a second Antique spoke "No, Friends, let her conclude. The volunteers went through tough times to collect this valuable information out there in the wilderness, the least we can do is listen to what they have discovered. Let's keep our minds open for a little longer."

"Thank you, Colleague. We are simply reporting what we found out there in the savannahs," reasoned the Providant. "Once we put everything together, we can make more informed decisions."

She looked around her. There seemed to be grudging consent, so she recommenced.

"It's evident that, like the Savants, the Dominants also fall into the Control seeking group, but in its more extreme iteration. They wished to exert power and manipulate other ants. And brute force was certainly one aspect of their behaviour, it's true. Interestingly, we also observed that far greater numbers of clans were joining the Dominants than were joining other groups. We are not sure why this may be; perhaps they sensed a logic to fighting fire with fire. Or perhaps they felt a more visceral need for protection.

"It was definitely nerve-wracking for our volunteers to meet and talk with these Dominant ants, many of whom had intentionally self-styled into gangs…

the Tyrant, the Virulant, the Violant, the Rampant, the Malevolant, the Assailant, the Arrogant… just a few of many we met. Their intention was to be fearsome; to evoke dread and foreboding. Can we really blame them for these confrontational tactics given the conditions they are living through?

"And despite their combative stance, many were surprisingly eloquent about their outlook. They told our volunteers they felt no embarrassment in being seen as powerful, superior, intimidating, aggressive and cunning. Quite the opposite in fact. They behaved lawlessly and unpredictably with little restraint or reason in their actions, and saw all of this as necessary and even honourable in their pursuit of survival."

"Not much fun or education with these ants," shouted a Coherant. "Where's the respect or contribution or empowerment or levity among these controllers? At least the others offered that. It seems all these Dominants are doing is creating fear and hierarchy."

"Once again, Friend, we ask you to withhold your judgment," said the young Providant quickly, aware of a rising buzz in the chamber. "As reckless as this behaviour might appear on the surface, there is another side. It has to be said that these ants also displayed impressive disciplines: not least a strong loyalty to their own, and an immense courage to face head-on the many crises which surrounded them daily.

"Going forward, and under different living conditions, their combative nature could quite feasibly be harnessed in some way and used as a protective force. Or it's quite possible they may yet possess many other strong attributes that we have not observed, or have not surfaced or matured during these fraught times. These attributes we can surely draw from once we can create a balanced dialogue among the groups.

"What is more, you must remember that you, the Coherant are already a highly advanced supercolony. We understand your ancestors conceived and enacted a Charter many, many generations ago to create and safeguard the lives you all enjoy now. You have built a wonderful community from the act of welcoming millions of migrants to share their skills and cultures with yours. We know of no other colony that can claim the privileges you take for granted.

"It is little wonder that you identify more with the Accepting and Growth perspectives I have described so far, and less so with the Control perspectives (and the Exposed perspectives yet to come). Perhaps predictably, as we audited the entirety of Coherant habitants here on this vast rock outcrop, we encountered far more of you who would likely fit the profile of Vibrants, Servants, Brilliants, Exuberants and even Savants.

"It's true we didn't find so many amongst you all here displaying Dominant, Dissonant and Truant behaviours, but there are certainly some. Not large numbers of you, but a presence nonetheless. And in their own ways, they contribute much to the social fabric of our community, perhaps in ways that are not immediately apparent. We urge you not to make comparisons or overlook just how fortunate you are; your living conditions are so much more sheltered and peaceable than the vast majority of ants out there on the savannahs.

"The Coherant supercolony is well-known and widely respected for being extraordinarily open-handed and inclusive compared to other clans and colonies. From our outreach audits we are convinced that this is a golden opportunity. If you so choose, you can consolidate this magnanimous outlook and create the vision that Anthea and so many of your antkin aspire to once and for all.

"You have the chance to seal the Coherant legacy by accepting not just the ants with whom you identify but those with whom you do not - yet. We urge you to welcome those with whom you feel at odds. Welcome those who see delights in areas where you currently see none. Welcome those whose instincts are different to yours. Seek to find the gifts they may yet bring to you. There is always something unforeseen we can find in others that can make us more complete."

This time when she finished there was complete silence, almost as if what she had recounted sounded so shocking - (or inspiring perhaps?) - that the assembled ants couldn't quite find words to immediately comment. "I'll tell you about the Truants and Dissonants now then, shall I?" the Providant offered, "and then we can move to discussion."

This time there was no reply from the crowd, so she quickly continued her review.

The Dissonants

"So, as you now know, we identified a further group with an **Exposed** and vulnerable perspective and named them the **Dissonants**," she began.

"The Dissonants we encountered entered conversations from a wholly unaware standpoint. Mostly negative and pessimistic, they were adept at finding 'buttons to push' with a view to goading other ants towards defensiveness. They demonstrated low levels of self-discipline and lacked willpower to follow through with challenging tasks. This led to repetitive and addictive behaviour, which in turn created an obvious and vivid social immaturity.

"When challenged, they were mostly petulant and tense, unpredictable and manipulative in their responses. It was difficult to pin them down to a definite promise or transaction, and we regularly observed them changing the parameters of an agreement by resorting to a nit-picking, over-literal account of what they had and had not agreed to.

"As a result, other ants often found themselves 'treading on eggshells' around them, since typically, Dissonants seemed to find more comfort in creating tension, rather than defaulting to a more mature social standpoint. As a result of all this rejectionist behaviour, others were wary around Dissonants, and they found themselves isolated and with little support or close friends.

"We would summarise their behaviour as immature, feisty, inconsistent, big-headed, small-minded, obstinate, cynical, quarrelsome and passive-aggressive. Such provocative behaviour makes for a precarious attitude to survival, and we felt this group was the most likely to find themselves under attack from marauders."

"These are the worst yet," called out a Coherant. "How would any of us agree to work alongside such obnoxious ants? Or to shelter them in our colony? I think we can do far better than this."

A number of ants voiced their thoughts, shouting over one another.

The Providant waited until the noise began to diminish, before attempting to reason with the crowd. "Friends, I ask you again to remember once more, these are siege responses. You can see just by this short presentation how immediately vexed you yourselves have become. These Dissonants are living in this state every single day. Let's choose to search for what may be positives in their survival approach, rather than what is contentious. I'd like us all to be able to discuss this in the context of all eight behaviours, to see what may emerge that may be useful to us. Please stay patient, I still have the last group to highlight for you."

The crowd was growing noticeably more restless and impatient. The Providant grabbed her moment.

The Truants

"Friends, we also became aware of groups of ants who seemed to want to live almost invisibly and without responsibility where possible, while, paradoxically, their one aim in life seemed to be to gain recognition; both are surprising attributes to find in any ant.

"This group we named the **Truants**, quite obviously in the **Exposed** group, and who appeared to be doggedly disinclined to engage with others as equals. They were clingy and needy, desperate for things to go their way - somehow, anyhow - and were stuck with the limiting belief that situations and decisions - including living or dying - are out of their hands.

"One shared with us the risky and fatalistic outlook

which typified Truants: 'We must simply reconcile ourselves to keeping a low profile and do what we can to make the best of what life throws at us. Life happens to us; it is what it is. We only have limited ability to influence things'. Truants tended to believe that they are ill-equipped to make any impact on the world around them.

"For them, to survive meant to submit, and they had long ago accepted it was preferable that their lives were organised for them by other ants, and would work hard but without passion, to fulfil others' expectations of them.

"Their language was bland, repetitive and mostly monosyllabic, and they were timid and resentful of others' abilities to expand a viewpoint or see it from other angles.

"It goes without saying that the Truants were the most negative and down-trodden of all the groups we encountered. However, on the positive side, they were hard-working, reliable and honest."

***

"Well, I'd prefer them to the Dominants," called out an ant from the back of the assembly.

"I agree," replied another. "Teach them a little self-confidence. They'll probably change, given time."

"Well, that's all of the groups, everyone, thank you so much for your attention," concluded the Providant. "Let's break out and discuss. All your perspectives are valued, please make your views known to the Antiques at the back of the chamber."

She looked around, trying to mask her relief at finishing her presentation. In the main, she sensed approval - the younger delegates in particular appeared impressed and excited, ready to embrace the possibility of new inaugurants. Impromptu groups formed to share their thoughts and ideas. The chamber hummed as the Coherant discussed what they had heard. The Antiques were impassive as they filed away to the far end of the chamber to confer amongst themselves.

Chapter 9 - Antiques oppose the vision

Anthea stood anxiously in silence with the Providant and the Antenna. Creating just eight survival groups from the consolidation of so many siege behaviours during their expedition had seemed like such a breakthrough moment. They had been sure the Antiques would see the potential in adapting these behaviours to form the basis of a new community leadership framework. They would surely be euphoric...wouldn't they? It had not occurred to Anthea that the Antiques might disregard them altogether.

Now, as the Antiques conferred, and the Coherant crowds held animated discussions across the chamber, Anthea could discern no obvious leaning towards acceptance or rejection of her vision. The Antiques looked inscrutably at each other as they debated in hushed tones, occasionally calling for other Coherant to join them. Anthea realised that she might have to justify its implementation far more robustly than she had at first envisaged.

James Mackenzie Wright

At length, one Antique stepped away from the huddle of elders and walked towards the stage. The room hushed and the groups of Coherant turned to listen.

"Colleagues," she said to Anthea and the Providant. "You have planned and executed an impressive mission to promote your vision to us. You, and all those who took part, are to be commended for your courage and selflessness. You have cast a bright light to illuminate the lifestyles of millions of our antkin in your quest for a social framework that can represent our reality.

"However," continued the Antique, "you are asking us to build an ever-expanding supercolony from tens of thousands and eventually millions of refugees, whose own communities would, at first glance, appear to be capitulating to segregation and disenfranchisement."

Anthea was tempted to confute but she wisely waited. This was not the way she had wished the presentation to be received, but she conceded there was some truth in the Antique's summary. She knew she would need time to collect and present her own thoughts clearly when the time came.

A second Antique spoke up. "It pains me to say what I must. Even as we are still beginning to understand what positive impact these siege tactics may provide to us, other alarming findings are revealed. You concede that these groups are not the finished product. If this is so, which appears indisputable from your presentation, how can you reasonably expect the Coherant to welcome into our ranks huge numbers of outsiders whose own image of themselves is incomplete and confused?

"And worse - far, far worse and certainly more difficult to rectify - this agitation seems to be leading to a situation where the various groups are considering themselves and one another to be more (and less) important. We are alarmed. It would seem you are asking us to become tolerant of the one thing ants should never tolerate: the blight of hierarchy."

Anthea looked towards the Providant group and gave a discrete nod. One stepped forward and spoke for them all.

"Esteemed Antiques, we anticipated this point, and we stand in full agreement with you. Hierarchy sires polarity wherever it raises its ugly head. Our bedrock focus since we accepted this task is that there should be equality among all ants. We Providant are resolute that any whiff of hierarchy in our societal support framework should never be acceptable. In this we know we have the firm support of the Coherant. Furthermore, we…"

"Be that as it may, Colleague," interrupted another Antique, abruptly, "while you have been away on your mission we have had time to appraise ourselves of the very real threats to our colony from closer to home. We all understand that the principal cause for the evolution of this unfortunate hierarchy situation stems from the unmet needs of the many itinerants desperately searching for their own security.

"Perhaps there are those fearing their original values won't be recognised, nor their voices heard? We have seen with our own eyes the roving, self-styled Dominant gangs of which you spoke. They have been openly encouraging unrest and swelling their ranks with ever more vulnerable ants whose own values and cultures are being steadily eroded by enticements of security and power.

"Allow me to quote from your vision, Anthea. You made a comment that we should attempt to create 'contentment and prosperity at levels so high as to eclipse any craving for conflict…to encourage friends and would-be enemies alike to find their own elevation by joining us rather than fighting us'. This is beginning to ring hollow when faced with these stark insecurities. These mobs are spreading disinformation, threats and doing everything they can think of to intimidate the smaller, defenceless clans. Fortunately, thanks to our own trained militants, we are able to stand our ground - for now.

"Your vision has become a much talked-about issue amongst many clans. As our Providant friend has graciously noted, we have a long and venerable history of welcoming and inaugurating diverse clans. We have reached this point of relative prosperity and security through our generous, though judicious, acceptance of outsiders.

"Your research asserts that all Coherant - indeed, that all antkind - can likely locate themselves within one or other of these survival behaviour groupings you have identified. If this is true, (and it may well be), are you also suggesting that we Coherant should harbour larger numbers of certain groupings, and less of others. If so, would it not be prudent to weed out the less desirable elements, rather than invite more in?

"Perhaps some of these survival behaviours may well be valuable to us. Some may not. But to accept all of them? And try to integrate them, and ask them to change their ways to our ways? Can we take that chance? Are we not encouraging an infiltration of antipaths and vigilantes who may well conspire to sow seeds of autocracy?

"Take this controlling group you name the Dominants, for example. Why would they not try changing the balance of what we have, when they deem the time is right? They could simply circulate rumours or fuel doubts around the likelihood of your all-encompassing Coherant vision becoming real.

"Or they could kindle civil unrest, or even instigate a full-blown insurrection, aiming to prove that antkind is inherently an aggressive species that can only respond to forceful rule. Their forceful rule, they will insist. Such unrest within our territories could lead to the creation of dozens, hundreds, maybe thousands of small-time, vicious, power-based clans, alongside which our more refined inhabitants would struggle to exist.

"For the moment such a calamitous projection is just that - a projection. The eventual consequences may be far less sinister than the dark picture we have painted. And then again, they may not. But either way, can we afford the time and resources to discover whether your proposal can indeed lead us to a more utopian vision of peace and prosperity? Perhaps, from weighing up the benefits and disadvantages of the insights the Providant have presented to us, we could conclude that we are, in fact, already safe enough?"

The chamber began to hum with the murmurs of the delegates, who were keen to debate this new angle. Anthea sensed a rising opposition to her proposal and realised she would have to speak up herself to defend her vision.

Chapter 10 - Anthea defends her vision

She stood up and cleared her throat.

"Esteemed Antiques, and friends. Please let us not move to catastrophise what has not yet transpired. Let us be clear: we are certainly proposing transition, and not status quo. Yet it may well be that a demotivation for my vision stems from what the Antiques have just outlined. It may well be that there is, as you say, something sinister already occurring. One thing is certain: we must not allow such concerns to smoulder, nor underestimate the unfortunate situation that might otherwise ensue.

"You highlight one group in particular - the Dominants - who are causing you some disquiet. It's true there are certainly ants out there who are displaying their inherent confrontational behaviours. Might we call these behaviours 'setbacks' rather than rush to elevate them to full-blown 'calamities'? We too noticed agitative behaviour among the Dominants, but also among Brilliants, Dissonants, Savants and Truants. In fact, even within our own Coherant colony we witnessed instances of ants within all behavioural groups appearing to let slip the high standards we have set ourselves. In these unstable times we must surely make allowances for such conduct, however frequent the lapses.

"You mentioned the blight of hierarchy. I too, share your concern in this regard, although I note you then go on to talk of 'less desirable elements'. We should be careful not to rush to judgment on the acumen of any group, nor whether one may be 'less' or 'more' desirable.

"And lastly, please don't overlook the plusses inherent in all the behaviours either. I concede both our siege mindset and our Charter have served us well up until now and kept us safe. Even, perhaps, *safe enough*, as you suggest. As we have explained, we are not intending to re-invent old behaviours; rather to re-explore them and set up ways to locate and distill their most beneficial elements. Our aspiration is to let go of the siege mindset and formulate a more contemporary, favourable one. In fact, I believe we should consider updating our very Charter itself."

An Antique stepped forward and raised a front leg. "Anthea, you and the Providant have presented your case, and we have listened," he said. "The information you have provided has given us much food for thought. However, I think I speak for all Antiques when I say that we still have strong concerns about the enormous number of migrants you are proposing we invite. Particularly with regard to safeguarding our current situation which, we all agree, seems more precarious than before. It would seem that you believe that an infinite influx of ants can render us immune to attack, regardless of their calibre, or what they may be able to offer us."

"I sense it is still the threat of hostilities which is weighing most heavily on your minds," replied Anthea. "Perhaps now would be a good time for us to seek insights from others too. Let us summon our learned anthropologists to determine the basis for this contention."

A number of anthropologists were called to the front of the chamber. Normally considered and understated, they were - on this point - blunt and unequivocal.

"Ants have evolved as marauders programmed with a ruthless DNA strand," their spokesant stated. "When we perceive ourselves to be under threat, this DNA strand compels us to attack strangers and even to turn in on those closest to us as a means to secure our own survival," they advised. "This aggressive streak, designed as it is with our self-protection in mind, will prove to be a stubborn trait to banish."

"Then this fight-for-survival reflex needs to be suppressed," added an Antique.

"Or could we instead say 'harnessed?' " countered Anthea. "Perhaps there is a way we could use it to our advantage. I am convinced we can create conditions which can offer security and comfort to all ants in need."

"But how, Anthea?" asked an exasperated Antique.

"I, for one, reject your fanciful vision that we can provide security for our colony simply by welcoming more and more peace-seeking but non-productive immigrants. And I know I am not alone. How would we know whether they were indeed peace-seeking? How could we ensure they would contribute to the colony? Anthea, we seem to be moving in circles - you surely remember we counselled against this scenario from the start."

"What if we were faced with newly-inaugurated ants openly regretting their recently acquired clanship?" asked a second. "Many appear already to be consorting in cliques, or solely with ants with similar attitudes to their own. There could be a real risk of permanent fragmentation from within."

 Ominously, a third noted, "With vast numbers of diverse and disappointed clans populating our colony, we could soon experience infighting on a scale we have never yet faced."

Anthea recalled that the Antiques had indeed predicted a state of potential overwhelm within their colonies from a vast and ever-increasing influx of immigrants.

"I have been thinking about little else throughout our mission," she replied. "May I steer you to the positive side? The revelation of the siege behaviours - as beneficial or as flawed as they currently may be - can provide a much-needed boost to the evolution of our own colony's social structures, productivity and confidence. They make us more aware of our own identities, both as individuals and as clans, and of what we could offer, given time.

"There is so much that is positive and well-meaning within them, though I concede too, that some behaviours also highlight our shortcomings. It seems that our peaceful philosophy has already been appreciated by many other clans who fully intend to arrive at our frontiers seeking inauguration. I sense your misgivings and that many of you are not in favour of my proposal. I ask, however, that you consider it without prejudice one last time, in the light of the longer term benefits that I am convinced will arrive for us all."

She stepped back. Surely they would see the big picture as she saw it? She had done and said all she could. Her future was now in their hands. Indeed, as Anthea saw it in that exact moment, so were the futures of all antkind.

Chapter 11 - Exodus

The Antiques returned to their huddle in the corner. This time, however, their decision was swift. They barely took the time to look to one another and nod before turning back towards Anthea and the Providant.

The most elderly Antique spoke for the group.

"Anthea. Venerable Providant. Your conduct and commitment to our colony has been exemplary. We are forever grateful for the dedication you and your teams of volunteers have shown to us all. We have made our decision. As it stands, your proposal presents too many question-marks that may compromise our safety. And that is, as yet, without allusion to the structured leadership components which you promised us. We are understandably nervous that this has not yet been presented.

"We are Coherant through and through. As such we are compelled to act with caution, prudence and forethought on behalf of our togetherness.

We cannot risk permanent fragmentation. We therefore cannot implement your vision. If indeed you feel you must remain committed to your path, Anthea, we feel we should ask you to step down as community strategist."

Anthea's heart sank.

"Esteemed Antiques," she replied, "I understand your need for a viable defence in the event of attack. I cannot in all good conscience condone the over-reliance on military solutions such as those you advocate because everything in my thinking tells me it is wrong to do so.

"We are all Coherant. And proud to be so. Being a Coherant has provided me with a safe and comfortable existence all my life, and I am profoundly grateful. You, as the elders of our colony, have guided us well through difficult times. We have achieved so much and pioneered new levels of inclusivity, tolerance and bonding amongst all our inhabitants, regardless of their origins. No other colonies that we know of have

James Mackenzie Wright

achieved this.

"But this inclusivity must extend to leadership, trust and decision-making too. It is true, you have put an exceptional trust in me, a younger ant, to contribute towards the organisation and forward planning for the colony. My question to you, though, is should my youth as a leader be exceptional? Ageing well is no prerequisite nor guarantee to leading well. This is perhaps where our thinking differs.

"The Providant have highlighted the immense pool of initiative and creative enterprise we already possess within our colony. Many of our inhabitants, old and young, would be willing to step up and contribute to the leadership, if given a chance. My vision would give a voice to every ant who wishes to take on the mantle of leadership - not just to elders.

"My intuition tells me that a policy of selective inclusion is unworkable. Either we are fully Coherant, in name and nature, or we are not. There can be no middle ground. I believe there is more to be gained for all of us were we to properly challenge our circumstances, embrace a new mindset, and find more ways we can evolve and thrive with a new Charter.

"Therefore, I can see only one solution. Were I to stay here, my views would be a constant distraction to the colony. So, from tomorrow, I will take my leave from the Coherant, wish you all well, and follow my instincts."

The Antique spokesant looked squarely at Anthea and straightened his back. He allowed a silence to pervade for fully twenty seconds. Then he spoke.

"If that is truly your decision, Anthea, then with heavy hearts we respect your integrity, and will not stand in your way. Your wisdom and devotion will always be admired, and you will be missed. May you find everything you need quickly, in your new life."

The Providant moved to stand next to her. "We have come to know and trust you without reserve during our mission together," they said, "and we would like to continue to build what we have started. We believe in your vision, and we shall stand by you as we create it together."

The Antenna too, walked over to Anthea. "Please allow us also to be part of your vision, Anthea. We shall journey alongside you willingly."

What happened next truly moved Anthea. One at a time, then dozens, then thousands of ants stood up and walked forward to join her.

"Your courage and vision have moved us greatly," they said. "You have moved us and inspired us to seek a new way. We too want the opportunity to create our own destiny."

Anthea smiled with gratitude. She addressed the entire chamber. "I thank everyone here today present for voicing their own truths. For those of us who wish to untether our desires and follow our imaginations, an unknowable journey awaits us all. Our nerve and resourcefulness shall surely be tested but we shall find a way. We shall leave at first light. All who wish to travel with us will be welcome. In anticipation, Friends!"

"In anticipation!" the excited breakaways roared back.

Anthea left the chamber to cheers and applause. Outside, she paused to look at the horizon. The setting sun splashed its rich evening palette across wispy African clouds, and she breathed deeply, filling her lungs with the warm air. Then she found an empty spot in the shade of a rock, lay down and closed her eyes. She was intending to meditate, but instead, fell immediately into an exhausted sleep.

Part II

New Beginnings

Chapter 12 - The Bund

The next morning, a vast contingent of excited ants had gathered at the Coherant boundary. A new life beckoned. The Antenna informed Anthea of a possible destination they had scouted during the earlier outreach missions. "On those same African savannahs where our ancestors first set foot, we discovered a bund flanked on two sides by water. Its situation could well afford us essential sanctuary from marauders," they told her. "It is two days walk from here, perhaps three, given the size of our travelling colony."

"Then that is where we shall head first," Anthea determined. And in minutes she had set off, with the massed cohort scrambling quickly to assemble and march behind her.

Three days later, the weary travellers arrived at the bund. Their spirits were immediately lifted when they saw it. It offered everything the Antenna had promised; narrow entrances at both ends of a raised causeway with fresh water on both sides, vast lush terrain for easy digging and plenty of shade from the savannah grasses and rocks. They spent many hours marvelling at every new aspect of this virgin territory which would become their new home.

Anthea called a meeting.

"Esteemed companions, we have done well to march for three full days in this heat. Such an enormous caravan was a provocative and exposed target for predators, and we have all arrived safely. This is a good sign.

"Make no mistake, this is no geographical fluke. The Antenna have once again excelled. This bund is an inspired choice made by strategic thinkers which will keep us all as safe as it is possible to be. The water surrounding the bund shall sustain us and keep our food supplies fresh. We have only two small land frontiers to defend, thereby freeing as many of us as possible to concentrate on building and federating new communities.

"During these unsettled times we shall continue to protect ourselves by merging our resources with as many ants as want to join us. Our first action will be to convene a new symposium and invite ants from far and wide. There we can fully debate all the observations from the previous outreach programme and listen to all your own ideas. Our vision will soon become our reality," she announced, to cheers from the crowd.

The symposium was organised and simply named - The Confer:Ants. It was widely advertised and hundreds of thousands of ants travelled to share their thoughts, experiences and wisdom. Even Anthea was surprised by the size of the appetite for a new way of living. It was a heady time, and they were exhilarated at the prospect of discovering how it might finally be possible to experience real security, prosperity and peace.

All the assembled ants accepted Anthea as the voice of the Confer:Ants and she assumed the role naturally.

"Companions - your combined thoughts matter strongly to us, and we will be grateful for your candour. We have made huge progress to even arrive here in the first place. With your help we can forge an exciting pathway to take all our lives forward. We shall present and explore four main themes during this Confer:Ants which shall last fifteen days and nights and culminate with the ceremony of our inaugural Integration Rite.

"We have debated long and hard about our new identity and I shall address this first. The following item will be our exciting new collective leadership framework. As some of you know, an impressive clan known as the Presidant have asked to join us and have offered to share their radical thinking on strong community building. Naturally, we have accepted, and they will soon be presenting their philosophies to us all.

"Once that is in motion, our volunteers shall outline the practical steps we shall take to prepare our new round of inauguration interviews, which will then be conducted over the next several days. Every single one of us shall be interviewed, as well as every single migrant wishing to join us - just as we had proposed to the Coherant. And lastly, the wonderful Mantra have requested to access these interviews in order to glean inspiration for a new anthem for our Charter. They will talk to us about this and it is intended that they shall unveil a new anthem for us all on the final day of this Confer:Ants during the Integration ceremony.

"So, esteemed companions, a truly trail-blazing Confer:Ants is in store for us all. I shall now open with our thoughts on identity."

Chapter 13 - Becoming Abundant

"Since we are soon to be an amalgamation of hundreds, and probably thousands of clans, it is indeed clear we are planning to form a supercolony that is likely to surpass the population even of the Coherant. Understandably, the same question arose in many of our conversations: What should we name ourselves?

"We have spent much time thinking about this. We all live together now on this bund, and we shall be inviting many, many thousands more to live with us. I am a child of Endurant parents and raised as a Coherant. Dual identity is a reality for many of us here - indeed the majority who have travelled to this Confer:Ants were born into other clans.

"Whichever clan we came from, we can never, and should never, forget our roots. We owe that to our ancestors who oftentimes underwent huge hardships to conserve our lineage. However, and I say this with the utmost respect to all who came before us, we are now here, together, to create a new and even greater chapter in our evolution.

"So, I can now call myself an ant of this bund - a bund ant. So are you too a bund ant, and you and you and you," she pointed out towards the ants present. "Every one of us here today, is, or desires to become, a bund ant. Each of us is the individual and the collective. So, at the end of our reasoning, we could find no more logical conclusion than that our identity, our supercolony shall be known as... Abundant."

The assembled ants looked to each other and repeated the name to themselves and to each other.

"Please stand if you wish to adopt this name as our identity," Anthea requested.

Every single ant in the chamber rose to its feet. "Then that name is carried," confirmed Anthea, to loud cheers. "From this moment on, we are Abundant!"

Chapter 14 - Building Community

"Let us now turn our thoughts to the issue of how we wish to design and implement a sustainable community leadership framework," Anthea resumed. "Many of us were present when we described the survival behaviours to the Coherant elders. You'll recall that many behaviours appeared awkward and, yes… frankly unacceptable in their raw state.

"Despite our entreaties for patience to allow us to work through some of these anomalies, the Antiques were unwilling to entertain the idea of inviting even more diverse and unknown groups of ants to join us and build together. At the time, although we challenged as hard as we could, it now seems we were fated to respect and accept their objections.

"With hindsight, I can now see that we, no… *I* made a significant oversight with regard to depicting the prevailing Coherant mindset and their Charter as templates for the whole of antkind.

James Mackenzie Wright

I continue to hold it as a truth that togetherness, inclusion and diversity are of paramount importance, and that the Coherant have been, and continue to be, extraordinary pioneers for us all. But we now know there are surely missing elements to those templates. I take responsibility too, for not outlining a strong enough link to leadership, as the Coherant elders had requested of us. I believe we are close to finding those elements here on our bund.

"In our preparations for this Confer:Ants, we have all reflected on the importance of a new social collective approach. With the benefit of more time, we have communicated those same eight survival behaviours to the President, for their contemplation, as well as our intentions for creating our own ideals.

"We indicated strongly that we wish to leave survival thinking behind and replace it with a newer, more expansive mindset. We asked the President to continue exploring those behaviours and to re-purpose them into a more collaborative, community leadership framework. We explained that, in time, as we all begin to feel more secure, we want to be able to recognise and choose how we can all best serve and contribute to our new colony. Each one of us, not just the elders.

"What the Presidant have designed is very exciting. We believe they have succeeded where we were unable, and we are truly thrilled with what they are about to present to you. Please welcome the Presidant to the stage so that they may share their thinking with you."

Anthea left the dais. A small group of Presidant stepped forward and one addressed the crowd.

"Thank you, esteemed companions, for the confidence you are according us. From the moment you communicated to us the eight survival behaviours you'd identified from your earlier outreach programme, it was obvious that many of the ants in each of those groups were conflating the purpose of their own roles with those of others.' Arbitrary and meritless hierarchies were forming and, worse still, were gradually being condoned, which contributed heavily towards the mayhem amongst so many clans.

"That these apparent siege hierarchies have been detected early has generally been accepted as a positive, in that it has allowed us to address them quickly. The consensus is that hierarchy of any kind shall never be allowed to destroy the Abundant legacy.

"Since we arrived on this bund, we have been asking all of you to explore your perspectives on how you all wish to live and work alongside each other. Indeed, alongside all antkind. Together, many of us have debated the suitability of those organic, often desperate siege behaviours. Certainly, leadership under peacetime is a very different concept to leadership under siege. Alongside the more antisocial aspects there were many potentially workable aspects too, and, as Anthea has hinted, we are pleased to say we have now been able to formulate a new adaptation. Gone is the fear and the strife to be replaced by peace and prosperity.

"So here before you all today, we would like to unveil our new and radical community leadership framework. It comprises a brand-new leadership outlook that we have re-imagined from each of the eight survival behaviours, and three essential working principles to accompany them.

"Our hope is that when these are fully understood and integrated correctly into our communities they will create optimum cohesion and productivity. Not only within our immediate community here on this bund, but also, as we learn to hone and embody them, we envisage that they can bind all antkind into a supportive, bountiful species wheresoever we colonise. Why wouldn't we aim for that, colleagues? Let us choose the stars we want in our firmament. Now is the perfect era for us to dream and innovate.

"Gradually, when we began to adapt and repurpose each survival behaviour to fit a more progressive and productive community mindset, we were persuaded that eight groups working holistically was an optimum number in terms of efficiency. So we kept the number and behavioural framework, renamed them 'Community Octants', and gave each its own eponym to better reflect the social outlook and purpose it represents.

"We believe that whilst every ant can possess an affinity of sorts with any of the eight new Octants, they are designed so that each of us will experience a precise, clear and instinctive alignment to just one. The Octant to which we feel most naturally compelled is most likely the one in which we will work most productively and feel most fulfilled.

"Our suggestion is that, once we fully understand how to work with them, every Abundant will adopt them as the epitome of ants' highest functioning. A confident knowledge of all Community Octants and their guiding principles will also allow you to reflect on your own purpose within the colony. Most of us should find ourselves drawn to our most preferred Octant fairly quickly.

"You may perhaps be asking yourselves, 'How will I know how to choose the right Octant for myself?' Well, if you will accept to work with us, we will assist every single one of you, (and over time, every future inaugurant too), in choosing the Octant that feels most apt for you. Then we can bring you to the fullest awareness of the duties and commitments associated with your chosen Octant and commence a robust and bespoke mind-elevation to every ant.

"Working together, all eight Community Octants comprise our new collective leadership framework. So here they are, in random order. Please note the Octants are conceived to be co-equal and to co-exist with no hint of a hierarchy amongst them. Take note of all eight and see where your inclination leads you."

Chapter 15 - The Community Octants

The Congruants

"We will start with the **Congruants**. From the multiple pockets of Servant behaviour that the Providant identified, we found much that was positive to glean from them. They were principled and virtuous - an outlook that had kept them relatively safe over generations. Many of their behaviours are built into this **Congruant** Octant.

"Perhaps the Servants' main downside seemed to be that they had attracted a reputation as being too distant and detached from the everyday dramas of colony life, and therefore found building strong relationships difficult. Other ants reported feelings of inferiority around their air of apparent irreproachability.

"These are easy characteristics to adapt into a positive perspective. We have re-shaped these into the **Congruant** Octant whose social outlook is Pastoral and whose purpose is to support and encourage. The **Congruants**' defined mission is to intuitively enable others to grasp life skills and concepts. They have talents for demonstrating belief in every ant and for creating learning through the experience of successes and failures. They will be responsible for setting up challenging tasks so ants can explore their motivations towards essential colony roles."

The Compliants

"Then there are the **Compliants**. This Octant is a re-vitalised version of the Truants, whose siege mentality was perhaps the most fearful of all the behaviours identified by the Providant. The Truants' least useful tactics were to assume a state of powerlessness and invisibility, and these we have transformed. What we could develop was their loyalty, sense of duty and tireless work ethic, all of which are indispensable when safeguarding a colony.

"The social outlook within the new-look **Compliant** Octant is Loyal. Their purpose is to serve and protect and their defined mission is to work in accordance with established colony guidelines and norms. They will be responsible for building and maintaining nests, foraging for food and guarding the colony and Queens from danger."

The Mantors

"Then there are the **Mantors**, whose social outlook is Educational. Their purpose is to guide and elevate. The **Mantors**' defined mission is to research widely and disseminate useful information to the colony so ants become curious, aware and inspired.

The **Mantor** Octant is based on the more positive aspects of the Savants whom, we noticed, had assumed a cultural high ground with their undoubted knowledge and informed views on most topics. Savants were expert, intellectual and engaging, straightforward, amicable and articulated and we have recognised and prioritised these values within the **Mantor** Octant. The Savants' less amenable characteristics - being somewhat evangelical, judgmental and pompous - no longer have a place; the **Mantor** is predominantly an educative Octant."

The Resiliants

"The **Resiliants** are next and their social outlook is Organisational. Their purpose is to coordinate and mobilise. The **Resiliants**' defined mission is to protect the colony and maintain discipline in the work force, and their responsibility is to ensure every team is working cohesively and at its most efficient. This Octant has emerged from the often unsavoury antics exhibited by the Dominants (and the sycophants they surrounded themselves with). Much of their siege behaviour was antipathic in the extreme; aggressive, manipulative, ruthless, argumentative, unpredictable and lawless."

"This group will likely need the greatest mind-elevation effort to allow these behaviours to disappear. One of the Dominants' more positive behaviours, however, was their ability to create and enforce strong boundaries, disciplines, rules and decisions. This we shall certainly adapt and embed within the role of our **Resiliant** Octant."

The Bon Vivants

"Then we have the **Bon Vivants**. They share many characteristics with the Exuberants, who were always motivational and uplifting. We have tasked the **Bon Vivants** to keep a perspective on the 'bigger picture', (a quality the Exuberants occasionally seemed to lack). Their social outlook is Motivational and their purpose is to lighten and brighten. The **Bon Vivants**' defined mission is to maintain morale and provide well-being contributions to alleviate ants' daily stresses. They are responsible for connecting ants with their lighter sides, taking their minds off the difficult parts of their work and letting off steam as they need to."

The Illuminants

"Many of the siege attributes of the Brilliants are useful to this next Octant. The Brilliants were altruistic and outward-looking, ingenious and

pragmatic, while unafraid to make mistakes.
On their downside, we observed disappointing
listening skills, over-confidence and their stubborn
insistence on promoting their own ideas, regardless
of others' views. So, by sidestepping those, we
have introduced instead a more measured, less
reactionary stance and named this Octant the
Illuminants. Their social outlook is Inspirational
and their purpose is to innovate and solve. Their
defined mission is to design and implement clever
solutions to difficult situations."

The Defiants

"To create the **Defiant** Octant we closely studied
the Dissonants and their interesting siege tactics.
Since they were so intent on not conforming to
established ways of doing things, they often found
themselves shunned by just about every other
ant. We realised that by steering their obvious
energies into a more healthy and strident curiosity,
they could actually turn out to be very useful to a
colony.

"The Dissonants had perfected a sulky deference and pessimism as their principal survival strategies and were woefully un-self-aware, so these were qualities which we reimagined and elevated into a respect for oneself and others. From this we conceived the **Defiants** Octant whose social outlook is Practical and whose purpose is to challenge and explore. The **Defiants**' defined mission is to call into question accepted ways of doing things, and to find what is not apparent in what appears obvious. They shall be responsible for coming up with ever new and safer ways of organising a colony."

The Radiants

"The last Octant are the **Radiants** whose social outlook is Spiritual and whose purpose is to model forbearance, joy and health. The **Radiants**' defined mission is to provide universal oversight and support to every ant who requires it. They derive from the Vibrants who, as you'll recall, were able to display a remarkable lack of concern around the obvious dangers they faced daily and behaved serenely at all times.

"The Vibrants' principal contribution to those around them was this inspirational sense of calm they exuded, rather than any tangible or practical offering. As a result, other ants were not entirely sure how to relate to them. In this new guise of **Radiant**, however, we are convinced of the need for this spiritual guidance to balance the harshness of everyday toil in our colonies."

James Mackenzie Wright

Chapter 16 - Guiding Principles

The Presidant continued.

"As a follow-on to the profound work already achieved at this Confer:Ants we have also conceived three underpinning principles. These are indispensable to the implementation of the Community Octants. Here is a brief outline of each principle - we can expand your understanding of them in due course.

- "The principle of **Reciprocal Respect** demands that every Community Octant be seen as equal, esteemed and pivotal to the survival and growth of the colony.

- "The principle of **Default Aspiration** demands that we ants must aspire to just be what the colony needs us to be, accepting our place and purpose in the colony with gratitude and without complaint.

- "The principle of **Engaged Disengagement**

demands that we trust every other ant to fully engage with the tasks required by its Octant. This allows us to disengage from task overlap, meddling and scrutiny of others, thereby liberating us from judgment.

"We appreciate there is a lot to take in. If you accept, we will commit to embed these Octant principles within every single Abundant and to ensure the mantles of social responsibility are fully assumed."

The spokesant stepped back to join her peers. Anthea resumed her place in centre-stage.

"We are grateful to the Presidant for their industrious efforts and their offer to work with us all," she said. "When we first met them, we were struck by their unique and noble social outlook. Notably, they indicated they have no aspiration towards a permanent authority, preferring instead to 'preside', (to guide and oversee), as and when a situation requires their particular expertise - as their clan name implies.

"They recommended their concept of presidantcy - one in which any ant is at ease holding the status of presidant, and only for as long as its particular expertise is required by that situation. Each can expect to be nominated *temporarily* as a presidant at any time - this is already commonplace within their day-to-day interactions. At all other times each ant gladly supports the presidantcy of others. This sounds like a leadership philosophy at its most pure - ***every ant leads, every ant follows***.

"They asked us whether we would consider exploring this concept in conjunction with the Octants. Let us put it to the vote. Who wishes to accept their offer of exploring these Community Octants with the intention of embedding them as the framework for our new collective?" Anthea asked.

An elderly participant spoke up in a firm voice from the crowd: "These new Octants sound sensible and logical, with no rough edges this time - a big improvement on those survival behaviours. And what's more, the President appear to me to be highly capable and gifted tutors. I for one, am intrigued to understand more. We should realise that this could potentially be the last constructive decision we might have a chance to make as a colony. If we don't act soon, any colony we build could easily be annihilated by marauders from outside, or indeed, gradually decimated from within. My vote is to work with the Presidant. Who is with me?"

Once more, the consensus was instant and unanimous. Every ant stood up tall and raised their front two legs in assent.

"So shall it be," determined Anthea. "This Confer:Ants has voted to entrust our social outlook to the Presidant, who shall soon, themselves, be inaugurated amongst the first Abundant. We look forward to adopting their Community Octant framework for the advancement of our Abundant supercolony.

"Over time, the Presidant will continue to spread the Abundant message, via this framework. Our mindful conviction is that Abundant colonies can proliferate and self-sustain once all inaugurants accept their true purpose. Meanwhile, let us publicise our vision across the savannahs and beyond, and welcome the antworld to our bund. We shall prevail, dear Abundants. Once more, in anticipation!"

"In anticipation!" the crowd roared back.

Chapter 17 - The Abundant Charter

The mood in the chamber was expectant, as the inaugurants waited for yet more life-changing pronouncements.

"Much work has taken place for us to arrive this far. Now we shall focus on the interviews and the Octant education initiative," Anthea said. "In less than two weeks we have planned that our inaugural Integration Rite is to take place, to formalise the existence of our new Abundant supercolony.

"We have our Abundant name, but our identity is more than just a name. With the help of the President, each one of us will soon be able to define our individual purpose and contribution within the colony," Anthea continued. "And of course, we are fortunate to have among us the thousands of seasoned, highly trained volunteers from our earlier mission, and we will be training thousands more. We have tasked them with an audit to conduct new interviews with every single ant wishing to become Abundant.

"Strong solutions are born of strong questions, so the volunteers are already honing rafts of searching questions before the audits begin, which will be immediately following this Confer:Ants. They will elicit anything and everything that works and that doesn't, with no judgment, critique or blame. We want the best ideas, regardless of who brings them. We forecast that these interviews will yield fascinating and far-reaching insights which will be of great benefit to us all.

"And lastly, we have commissioned the venerable and much-admired Mantra clan to update the Charter that many of us will remember from our days with the Coherant. They will now introduce themselves."

An eclectic group of ants marched neatly on to the stage, saluted, and all but one took two steps backwards to leave their spokesant in centre-stage. The Mantra addressed the crowd with no preamble.

"You will be seeing much of us in the coming days, Friends. We shall be everywhere', announced the Mantra. "Our fixation is on selecting from the interviews, any and all questions, responses, insights and ideas that instinctively ignite our appreciation. We are looking for the incisive, the piercing, the wise, the crafted, the whimsical and the downright perspicacious. We have been asked to fashion your words into a most potent and enduring composition.

"It has been proposed that the new Abundant Charter, shall be rewritten to exist under a banner of Collective Leadership. The Charter's philosophy shall be '**Every ant leads, every ant follows**' (inspired by the Presidant), which shall be woven into the Octant Leadership framework and its guiding principles which the Presidant have also designed.

"Our contribution shall be an anthem known as The Covenant and shall form the final part of the Charter. This shall become irrevocably associated with the Abundant, and eventually known to the whole of antkind.

"The Covenant will take the form of a pledge to which all soon-to-be inaugurants shall commit themselves as they become Abundant. You, we, and many, many more like us shall recite the Covenant as the crowning moment of our Integration Rite.

"Until soon, Friends."

He stepped back to join his clan, and they all turned as one to their left and marched off the stage.

Anthea resumed her place and continued. "We are grateful to the Mantra who will be working closely with the volunteers during all interviews. Let us now focus on the interviews and the Octant education programme - please make yourselves available over the next few days for both."

Chapter 18 - The Interviews

The next days of the Confer:Ants were intense but morale on the bund was sky-high. The volunteers began their undertaking to identify how ants from all clans perceived their pathways leading towards (and away from) harmonious integration. Residents and migrants alike were encouraged to contribute their own thoughts and wisdom for the creation and expansion of the Abundant supercolony by being showered with a multitude of questions. Many of the answers delighted the Mantra.

For example, to the volunteers' question, 'How do we convince ants to share of themselves?' they appreciated a contemplative reply from some Benevolants: 'Sharing requires nothing but ease with our wholeness. Whether we receive anything in return matters little, since we are already complete.'

"Sublime!" they mused.

To, 'How can we find what really matters?' the

James Mackenzie Wright

Significant provided a most elevated response: 'What truly matters to us is our conviction that insurmountable barriers... are not.'

And to, 'How can we know whether success is achievable?' the Expectant were very pragmatic: 'Where unfaltering intentions meet unwavering resolve - success is an inevitability'. "So deep, so powerful!" the Mantra enthused.

Later, to, 'How valuable is diversity?' it was the Stimulant who caught their attention by replying: 'There is value in the uncommon, the unlikely, the unusual, the quirky and things as yet untried. But of more value still is the courage to embrace them.'

And to, 'How do we best learn?' the Observant's perspective excited them greatly: 'To listen with one's fullest attention is a generous gift - ever rewarded with the deepest of learnings.'

To, 'Despite our size, how can we walk tall?' the Eminant clan were poetic and emphatic: 'Where self-belief flows, antkind grows'...

…and many, many more.

"These are exquisite!" cried the Mantra. "These and so many other responses have inspired us. Please keep them coming and we shall continue to spend our time in urgent and diligent craft to create the Covenant".

It became second nature for the volunteers to formulate ever more acute and profound questions to ask during the interviews…

- "What does being Abundant mean to you?"

- "What can you contribute to enhance our positive impact on the world?"

- "How do you see Abundants becoming an enduring force for good?"

- "What needs to happen to fully realise an awesome state of contentment?"

- "How would you compare your fortunes to those of other ants you encounter?"

- "What are some defining things about the clans you belonged to before inaugurating as Abundants?"

- "What worked well for you in your original clans, that could be reinstated in Abundant colonies?"

- "And what didn't work?"

- "What do you see as your purpose in life?"

- "How would you describe your social outlook?"

- "What do you notice about the behaviours and attitudes of ants from other clans towards you?"

- "Which Octant most naturally attracts you?"

…and the ants duly responded in kind, providing ever more acute and profound insights.

Chapter 19 - The Covenant

The day of the Integration Rite arrived. A sea of excited would-be inaugurants flooded the makeshift amphitheatre - an enormous natural rock cavern - offering welcome shade from the relentless sun and sandstorms that regularly swept across the bund.

A Providant opened the ceremony.

"Esteemed fellow ants. As all of us here present are aware, we ants are still a new species in search of ourselves. The aspiration of this Confer:Ants was to position Abundants as a vital force for good; exemplifiers of peaceful and productive living and of the very highest codes of moral values and behaviour. We all stand in anticipation of becoming Abundant.

"We have been impressed by the Presidant and our teams of volunteers as they have worked tirelessly on our education and interview programmes. Countless interviews and conversations have been patiently conducted by them with each one of us. Every response, idea and idiosyncrasy has been explored, appreciated, and exploited. We have mulled over the myriad potential ways of accomplishing your suggestions for creating a peaceful, enduring, prosperous and inclusive colony.

"We are grateful to our distinguished associates the Mantra, for their seminal work on The Covenant, undertaken on our behalf. We now eagerly await the unveiling of their work to conclude this ceremony. It just remains for us all to pledge ourselves to the Abundant way," she said, turning to acknowledge the Mantra. "Let the Mantra conclude the inauguration with their truly touching and powerful pledge."

The Mantra took their place centre-stage and a spokesant stepped forward. "We offer this opus as a cherished definition of all that is Abundant. It shall be known as our Covenant, and we introduce it for you now. May it serve and guide every ant here present, and all antkind, in perpetuity.

"With your interviews behind you now, we invite every ant wishing to join the Abundant supercolony to recite, and in all ways to embody this Covenant. During this Integration Ceremony all of us shall pledge to uphold its exemplary standards. We shall each provide our personal guarantee to donate whatever assets and strengths we possess to support the Abundant cause.

"I, and two colleagues, have the immense privilege to ask you all to stand and repeat The Covenant."

Several hundred thousand ants rose as one.

The Mantra spokesant was joined by two more Mantra. They paused to appreciate the gravitas of the moment. Then they intoned in unison:

"I am Abundant…"

"I am Abundant…" the inaugurants repeated.

"I stand in the knowledge…"

"I stand in the knowledge…"

James Mackenzie Wright

"… that our lands are bountiful and overflowing with more than we need…"

"…that our lands are bountiful and overflowing with more than we need…"

The litany continued with the massed inaugurants repeating every new line:

…I share what I have in support and protection of any ant in need

…I work relentlessly for the things that matter

…I expect to excel and expect others to expect me to excel

…I appreciate the worth of unorthodoxy and idiosyncrasy

…I search for opportunity and learning from any source

…I respect and ignite the thinking and endeavours of others

…I walk tall, confident that I am enough

…I bring lightness and grace to wherever it is absent

…I am as content for the good fortune of others as I am grateful for my own

…My self, my work, my life - Abundant, always.

…I am Abundant!

…I am Abundant!

…I AM ABUNDANT!"

The last line was roared out to deafening cheers. The first Abundant supercolony was born.

Chapter 20 - Abundant, always

As the noise subsided, a Providant walked on to the stage alongside the Mantra. She waited for quiet before speaking.

"Friends, we recognise all those of you who have believed in the Abundant vision to the extent that you have risked everything to travel to this bund. We have been both humbled and astonished at the solidarity that we are all experiencing. We are convinced that the Abundant supercolony will continue to grow and mature. We commend you all for your moral fortitude and generous spirit towards the common goal. Being Abundant has truly become our reality - a most thrilling, a most vital way to live and thrive.

"All your wonderful, diverse, and imaginative thoughts, skills, attitudes and innovations are blending into a glorious melting pot. We are on the verge of producing the unique and bespoke representation of what we all seem to want most for Abundant living.

"But first let us hear from the most special, the most inspirational ant any of us have ever had the good fortune to meet. It is due to her vision and her courage that we are all assembled here, choosing to inaugurate as members of the world's first ever ant supercolony. Friends, I give you…Anthea!"

The chamber erupted. Stamping, calling, laughing; the crowd could sense the culmination of what was for many of them a lifelong ambition: peace, safety and prosperity.

For some minutes, no one made any attempt to quieten the euphoria. Eventually though, Anthea moved forward to speak and waited respectfully until the assembly fell silent.

"Dearest Abundants," she began, and paused, a little overcome. "Abundant. It is wonderful to hear myself say this name - our name - and to see the embodiment of all that it represents standing before me. I want to thank you all for supporting this sensitive and controversial pathway. It has no precedent, as the Coherant Antiques pointed out, and as such it constituted a massive risk to you all. There could have been rebellion and new fragmentation, but you have made it otherwise. Our hope was that as Abundants we all would come to view this path as a virtuous and laudable one. It certainly appears now that we have.

"Thousands of clans have chosen to join us, and today we can truly claim to be a supercolony. Probably the first to assimilate such a huge endorsement from such a diverse base. Together we can continue to mastermind our growth and prosperity.

"The astute Consultant chose well in engaging the Providant - both clans now inaugurated as Abundant, of course. To both, we owe a huge debt of gratitude - maybe even our lives. The Providant rose instinctively to the occasion with their firm, diplomatic and sensitive persuasion of the early bund ants to accept ever more immigrants. They have proved themselves to be deft, dignified champions of the vast immigrant gene pools that our Abundant colonies have inherently become.

"Due most likely to our colony's size, tenacity and regimen we no longer find ourselves under serious threat of attack. Our identity seems strongly defined. Let us look at what it means to be Abundant.

"We have an Abundant philosophy; the epitome of pure leadership:

Every ant leads, every ant follows.

"We have a supportive Abundant community; coequal and collective:

The Congruants

The Compliants

The Mantors

The Resiliants

The Bon Vivants

The Illuminants

The Defiants

The Radiants

"We have Abundant principles; resolute and fair:

The principle of **Reciprocal Respect**

The principle of **Default Aspiration**

The principle of **Engaged Disengagement**

"We have our Covenant pledge; consummate and bold:

My self, my work, my life - Abundant, always"

She paused and looked around. A spontaneous murmur ran through the crowd. After several moments she asked simply, "But, Friends, what can we do with this? I ask you in all sincerity. What is truly the full extent of what we can offer to the world?" The assembled ants looked at each other in surprise. What might be coming next? they wondered.

"I believe this definition of our identity is magnificent. And yet, is it as expansive as it could be?" asked Anthea. "I have admitted I earlier believed that the Coherant Charter was a paragon. I believed I could simply transfer it to us as Abundants and continue on our journey. How wrong I was.

"So now here we are. We have built our own Charter; infinitely preferable to the last one. We have built our new supercolony. We are peaceable, productive, content and prosperous. But I ask again: What do we now *do* as Abundants? Are we to be more than just a definition?"

The assembled ants hadn't seen this coming and sat back, sensing more to come. They were becoming familiar with Anthea's tantalising orations now and knew she was building up to something. Inevitably, she didn't disappoint.

"What questions do we still need to ask to further advance our journey?" she asked them.

One bold ant spoke up. "Perhaps we need to ask how we can enable enduring peace within our colonies?"

"That's a key point," agreed Anthea, "and one we will certainly tackle in due course. But I think now we may need even bigger questions."

"How can we make sure we continue to act as role models so that all ants can live and work together and respect one another?" offered a second.

"That's better still," said Anthea. "And… can we be even more expansive?"

The Abundant crowd looked at each other. Usually they appreciated her incitements; at this moment they now seemed slightly apprehensive. Some shifted from leg to leg; a sure sign they were on edge. None, however, made so bold as to offer a new question.

Anthea took a long, deep breath. Silence had once again fallen on the crowd. Since no ant appeared ready to further the debate, she looked around, as if calculating the effect her next words were to have.

"As ever, in order to find outstanding solutions, some new, outstanding questions are needed," she said. "I envision that when we find such questions, and learn to embody their answers, Abundants shall become admired as prolific, influential, compelling ants, whose ethics and philosophies shall be esteemed and imitated for all time.

"If no-one has questions to offer, I have some. My instinct is that they may likely challenge our outlook to new limits. Do I have your permission to offer them to the assembly?"

More expectant hush from the chamber indicated the ants' assent.

"My fellow Abundants, I challenge us all here present, to be bolder, more daring and more presumptuous in our imaginations than we have ever been. My first question, that I ask to us all, is 'how far might we dare to presume?'"

"Would we dare to presume, for example, that we Abundants could eventually create a most prodigious and potent force, not just amongst ourselves, but amongst all antkind?"

"Or might we dare to presume influence not only across our beloved bund, not only across our magnificent Africa, but throughout an entire planet we have yet to conquer and colonise?"

"Might we further dare to presume that our Abundant mindset might one day be an inspiration not only to all of antkind, but to other species too?" she continued.

"Might we dare to presume, fellow Abundants, that in the future we might be hearing, no… that we should *expect* to be hearing our good name spoken and admired by every sentient being worldwide?

"Or still yet, that all sentient beings - those present and those still yet to appear on this planet - will one day adopt our Abundant principles and philosophies to define their own daily aspirations?"

There was visible consternation in the chamber. No ant had ever seriously entertained these thoughts before. Colonising a planet…? Becoming a beacon of virtue for other ants was one thing, but for other species too…?

She was definitely beguiling them all that day, taunting and mesmerising them (and probably herself too), with the passion in her words. None could possibly have been aware of the enormity of the planet that ants would, indeed, eventually colonise. Or that new species would indeed evolve and adopt Abundant thinking. Yet Anthea was somehow foreseeing it all. Her questions were undeniably calculated to envision their life paths more clearly than anything before.

She paused, trying to gauge whether she was overstepping the mark. Her eyes were bright and excited. She was enjoying herself. She raised her thorax to project her voice louder and clearer than ever. Her last, most audacious and rousing call-to-arms left them giddy with excitement.

"Friends, we are Abundant!

"Abundant - the living embodiment of all that is bounteous, prolific, complete, and inexhaustible.

"Abundant - the definition of all that is optimal and aspirational.

"Abundant - the most noble and glorious way of living that one can imagine.

"I, Anthea, stand before you all here present, daring to presume that Abundant shall come to mean precisely this."

She paused and stood on her back legs to look out over the chamber. She sensed the excitement amongst the ants gathered there. Small cheers and applause broke out in pockets around the chamber. Seconds later, the whole chamber erupted with Abundant rapture as the magnitude of her message began to sink in.

Anthea smiled out at them and nodded benignly. She made no effort to contain the euphoria; the spontaneity of the moment was too precious and valuable to every ant present.

Chapter 21 - Anthea Rests

And indeed, so it came to pass. An enviable aura of calm settled over Abundant colonies as they spread quickly across Africa and beyond. Despite the continuing tumult elsewhere, Abundants reported that they felt more secure and able to relax in their lives and work. The huge and continuous influx of peaceful and productive inaugurants reassured them and satisfied their exhortation for safety in numbers. If there had been any remaining doubters, they soon appeared to be won over.

The timing too was fortuitous. The Abundants' remarkable evolution played out unchecked for another hundred million years or so during the magnificent Mega-Gigantica Era. The most conspicuous Mega-Gigantics with whom they shared the planet were clumsy dinosaurs who largely left them alone. Other more volatile gigantics (including you humans) were still, thankfully for ants, many tens of millions of years away from conception.

As Anthea had foreseen, the prodigious Abundants took full advantage of this halcyon age to concentrate on perfecting their masterful philosophy and culture. They steadily grew in number and became known for their respectful discipline, productivity and generosity. Inevitably, they found ways to travel away from the African savannahs to colonise and control *every land mass on Earth.

And Anthea?

It is said she lived an extraordinarily long life and found ever more innovative ways to travel the world to refine and spread her message. To be sure, there were many more twists and turns in her quest to establish Abundant thinking around the world, and these became well chronicled too. But she never wavered in her beliefs and optimism for the power and beauty of an Abundant mind.

*(except Ant'arctica. 'Arctica' in olden Semantic roughly translates as 'unwelcoming' and ants have stubbornly refused to ever set foot there).

"As I realised the vastness of the world out there, I wanted to make some sense of my place in it," she said. "I was born a child of the Endurant, learned much from the Coherant, but I have lived my best life as Abundant. Oh, how I have lived!

"Following my travels, I vowed to return to this very bund where I became Abundant. When the day comes, here is where I shall die Abundant, surrounded by my beloved antkin who have never failed to support and comfort me.

"Here, on this bund, is where I shall finish my work. I shall sit under these stones in the shade of these trees and tell Abundant stories to whomever wants to listen. I shall teach the lessons I have learned to bright, motivated young anthologists who can perpetuate them for future generations and broadcast them into mainstream Abundant culture. Our tireless itinerants can take responsibility for disseminating them to antdoms around the world.

"My intention has always been to deepen and share Abundant thinking to a point past antkind itself. We shall forever be sharing this planet with gigantics and sentient beings of all descriptions and I want nothing more for us to arrive at a point where all species can integrate with us, and immeasurably enhance their own livelihoods. And, in doing so, they will undoubtedly enhance ours also.

"So here I am now, towards the end of that path. I like to think my life hasn't been lived in vain.

"My self, my work, my life - Abundant always."

Also by James Mackenzie Wright

Seven For A Secret

Kid Pro Quo